Don't Stop Retrievin'

Karen Ritter

Presentation by *BookLeaf Publishing*

Web: www.bookleafpub.com

E-mail: info@bookleafpub.com

ISBN: 9789360947477

First edition 2024

*This is dedicated to Bella and her career as
a Therapy Dog.*

A New Home

I am so scared.
For more than a year I loved my family.
Why was I sent away?
Did I do something wrong?
Everything has changed.
My new home is quite different.
I have two new brothers who look like me.
Will they accept me?
My new mom watches me as I search for a safe
place.
Under the coffee table?
Behind the big recliner?
She tries to comfort me.
Her touch is warm and her voice is soft.
But I know my life has been altered forever.

Sleep Comes Fast

It's getting dark outside and I'm still hiding.
My new mom made dinner.
I watch my new brothers eat from the safety of
the back of the recliner.
I'm very hungry, but I don't want to leave my
hiding spot.
My dish is within reach…maybe just one bite.
It's delicious and once I start eating I cannot
stop!
My tummy is full and now I feel sleepy.
I don't see a kennel.
Where will I sleep tonight?
Wait, where is everyone going?
My brothers just jumped onto a big bed.
My mom invites me to join them.
I jump onto the bed and my mom cuddles with
me.
I feel safe and sleep comes fast.

Walk On

Excited happiness fills the room.
My brothers just saw my mom with a leash in
her hand.
They run quickly to the front door where my
mom is waiting.
I hang back, not sure what to expect.
My mom is calling me to join them.
I am reluctant, but slowly move toward my
mom's outstretched hand.
She pats my head and, somehow, she attaches us
all together.
We are outside in a place I have never seen
before.
One brother walks on my right, the other on my
left.
I feel safe walking between them.
There is so much to see.
Many noises and smells assault my senses all at
once.
It's hard to take it all in.
I'm smiling as we walk on.

The Dreaded Car

I have always feared riding in the car.
My mom opens the car door and waits.
Despite her coaxing I don't want to jump in.
Mom helps me onto the back seat.
I am scared.
I try to jump into mom's lap while she is driving.
My mom is angry and raises her voice.
Now I'm in a harness on the seat.
I don't feel safe and I'm breathing fast.
I squirm onto the floor and lay down in the small
space behind the front seat.
It feels better, like I have walls around me.
Mom doesn't seem to mind so I stay there.
I exhale.
I am safe.

Pet Smart, Not Smart

Today we travel to place that has many moving cars.

Mom helps me out of the car but I am scared and want to get back in.

Mom walks with me to some glass that starts to move right in front of us.

I try to pull away but Mom urges me forward.

A range of smells assault my nose as we walk in.

We meet a stranger and I have to do tricks for her.

She sits me in a doorway, drops my leash, and tells me to stay.

My mom walks away.

When I hear mom calling me, I know I should run to her.

But I'm frightened and I run to the glass that moves instead.

Now I'm running toward all the moving cars.

My mom and the lady are running after me, yelling my name.

They catch me and I can tell they are distraught.

I hope I passed my test!

A Thief in Broad Daylight

My mom just got home and put some things on
the kitchen counter.
She goes into the garage and the door closes
behind her
Something smells wonderful.
No one is watching.
I put my front paws on the counter so I can
move my nose closer.
I cannot resist.
It tastes wonderful! So sweet and soft!
Mom just opened the door and saw me.
I quickly swallow the evidence.
I think I'm in trouble because her voice is very
loud.
She's slapping the counter and telling me no!
I'm outside again.
I think I made a big mistake.
Will she be mad at me forever?

Rope Toy Madness

Is that something new on the kitchen counter?
I can smell it.
I can't seem to contain my tail from quickly
moving back and forth.
My mom sees my excitement and asks if I want
it.
Do I want it?
Yes!
She tosses something to me that I've never seen
before.
It has strings and knots.
I start shaking it back and forth with intensity.
Now I'm running back and forth in the living
room throwing it in the air.
My brothers just look at me like I'm crazy.
Maybe I am.
This is the best gift ever!
My mom smiles as I entertain myself.
She truly loves me - life is good!

Training Terror

I'm standing in front of the big glass doors that
move again.
I don't want to go inside.
Mom does not let me resist.
We're walking to a little room in the back.
There are others that look like me in the room.
I avoid looking at them.
I don't want to interact with them.
Mom sits on a stool.
I try to squeeze underneath the stool to hide but
Mom won't let me.
She moves the stool and stands instead.
Someone is saying hello to everyone.
It's my turn and my legs are shaking.
She seems nice and her voice is soothing.
Maybe everything will be ok.

Getting Easier

I've been to the place with the big glass doors
that move many times now.
Every time I go it gets a little easier.
My legs no longer shake and I feel more
confident.
I love to see the nice lady every week.
She sits on the floor with me and rubs my ears.
I'm doing well walking through the isles.
But if see the doors, I want to run through them.
Mom now walks me to the doors and stops
before we can go through them.
I have to sit down and watch the doors open and
close without getting up.
This is very hard, but not as hard as it was at
first.
My mom is very proud of me.
She smiles and tells me I'm a good girl with a
happy voice.
That makes me happy too.
Our eyes connect and I smile back at her.

New Friends

There is a big commotion, but I don't know what
it is.
My brothers seem excited but I don't know why.
Suddenly I see a stranger by the sliding glass
door.
Should I sound the alert?
I look to my brothers for guidance.
They are clearly happy and do not bark.
The door opens and out rush two little animals.
Their energy is very high and everyone is
running circles around each other.
Mom comes outside with two strangers.
The woman has a ball!
I can always beat my elderly brothers to the ball!
With the first throw I learn that these new
friends are faster than me.
The competition is on!
I love these new friends!

Graduation Day

I'm back at the place with the big moving glass
doors.
I don't mind coming here now.
My mom keeps praising me when I'm here.
I must be doing something right.
Today feels different.
I'm being asked to do everything I've ever
learned.
I struggle to stay in place when my mom walks
away.
I can't do it on the first try.
We try again and I still cannot do it.
But on the third try I'm able to do it.
My mom and the nice lady are both clapping
their hands!
The nice lady is putting something she calls a
graduation cap on my head.
She is taking my photo, so I pose as proudly as I
can.
I heard that I passed with flying colors!

Loss

I am outside with my brothers.
I see my brother Rascal lying in the grass, not
moving.
I move closer because I feel something is wrong.
He tries to lift his head to look at me, but he
can't.
I'm worried so I lay down close to him to
comfort him.
Mom is finally home!
She opens the door, and calls to all of us, but
Rascal does not move.
Mom helps Rascal up and they disappear into
the house without me.
I hear Mom's car leaving again and she is gone
for a long time.
Mom is finally home.
Where is Rascal?
I am running all over the house looking for him
but I can't find him.
Mom is crying so I go to her to comfort her.
I don't think I will ever see my brother again.

Test Run

Mom asks me if I want to go for a ride?
A pink bandana is placed around my neck.
I'm very excited as I climb into the car.
We arrive at a large building.
There are so many people!
Everyone seems very excited to see me.
I love the warm touches as I move from person
to person.
One person seems afraid to pet me.
Mom turns me around backwards and he finally
touches my back.
I wait patiently as he begins to stroke my back.
Mom finally turns me around and he pets my
head.
Our eyes connect and he smiles.
I'm so happy that I won him over.
I feel confident and accomplished!

Test Day

Mom says today is a big test.
We are in the car for a long time.
When we arrive, someone is waiting for us with
a dog.
Then a woman joins us with a dog.
The scents in the building we enter are different
from what I've smelled before.
We walk into a room where people are sitting in
chairs that have wheels.
Others are sitting on regular chairs and couches.
Everyone seems very excited to see us.
We move from person to person to say hello.
Some people make happy noises as they pet me.
I move in closer and this seems to make them
even happier.
Before we leave, Mom holds my face, looks into
my eyes, and praises me.
Test day or not, I love making people smile!

Family Festival

I am in a big grassy courtyard today.
There are some people setting up activities
around the courtyard.
I hear that this festival is for homeless families.
I watch people line up at a gate.
I see children and that makes me happy.
When the gate opens, many children rush to me.
My tail is moving back and forth as they pet me.
Some are hugging me, so I lean into the hugs.
One little boy seems hesitant to pet me.
His mom coaxes him, but he hides behind her
leg.
He finally takes a step toward me.
I don't want to scare him, so I hold very still.
Our eyes meet and he places his hand on my
head.
His smile warms my heart!

A Slice of Happiness

Today I'm in another grassy courtyard.
Children are here with their moms, eagerly
waiting for me.
I hear someone say these families are victims of
domestic violence.
I know they have been hurt, so I will be extra
gentle today.
The children have big smiles on their faces.
They crowd around me.
I have many hands on me all at once, but I don't
mind.
I know they need some joy in their lives.
My mom invites the children's moms to pet me
too.
They also smile as they pet me.
My mom pulls out a laser pointer.
The children squeal and laugh as I chase the red
dot.
I'm very happy.
I was able to help them forget their hurt for a
moment.

A Cousins' Christmas

I have been in the car with my brother for hours.
I look at Mom with my best puppy eyes and she
says we'll be there soon.
When we arrive, I see the friends that visited my
home!
Wait, there are more!
Six us are now running around the back yard
chasing each other.
Is that a pool?
Mom tries to grab me and says no, but I jump in
anyway.
Now everyone is in the pool.
It's very cold, but I don't want to stop
swimming.
We can't go into the house because everyone is
drenched.
Towels appear and after intense rubbing we can
go inside.
It's chaotic as all six of us wildly chase each
other around the house.
I love playing with my cousins.
Best Christmas ever!

Champions

Today I'm at church with my mom.
Lots of people greet me when we arrive.
We enter a large building and I must sit quietly
while someone is talking.
After a long time, we move to a smaller room.
I'm so happy to see children here!
Some of these children hold me a little too
firmly.
It's fine because I've trained for this.
Sometimes kids with disabilities don't
understand.
I let them pull my ears and hold my face with
intensity.
One little girl talks a lot.
She seems to enjoy talking to me.
I sit quietly as she strokes me and tells me
remarkable stories.
Kids with disabilities are amazing.
To me they are champions!

Love Breaks Through

My mom has a friend we will visit today.
Her friend is very excited to see us arrive.
Mom and her friend talk while I wait patiently,
not sure why I'm here.
We walk into the Livingroom and it's suddenly
clear.
Mom's friend has a husband that is sick with
dementia.
I walk up to him, but he growls and shoos me
away.
After a minute I nudge his arm with my nose.
He pushes me away.
My mom sits next to him and asks him if he
wants to pet me.
He nods his head up and down.
Mom invites me to enter his space again.
She lifts his hand and places it on my head.
He smiles and begins to massage my head.
Love breaks through again!

Pure Joy

There are kids that live in poverty.
They cannot come to church, so Mom's friends take church to them.
When I arrive, the kids all scream with excitement and rush to the door.
My mom laughs and asks them to let us inside.
The kids have very high energy.
They are running circles around me, squealing with delight.
Many hands are touching me at once.
I am loving it!
My mom takes out the laser pointer.
I entertain everyone by pouncing on the moving red dot.
All the kids shriek and laugh as they take turns moving the dot around.
I don't disappoint them.
I'm happy that I can bring these kids smiles, laughter, and joy.
Pure joy.

Purpose

My Journey continues.
I have learned so much.
I know that I bring joy to others.
People smile when they see me.
I make a friend of everyone I meet.
My gentleness invites interactions.
My loving eyes bring calm.
I will nudge you if you stop touching me.
That often makes people laugh.
And sometimes there are tears.
I do not judge.
I am making a difference.
My life has purpose.
I am a Therapy Dog.